AF556079

LIFE LESSONS

'ONE WHO SERVES BECOMES THE MASTER'

India has produced some of the world's greatest religious leaders, sages, saints, philosophers, and spiritual thinkers. They were monks, nuns and renunciates, nationalists and reformers. No one religion had a monopoly on them. They range from Mahavira and Buddha, who lived over 2,500 years ago, to medieval saints like Chishti, Avvaiyar, and Guru Nanak, to more recent philosophers and religious icons such as Vivekananda, Ramakrishna, Saint Teresa, and many others. The spiritual and philosophical heritage they left behind is India's gift to all Indians and the world.

In the 'Life Lessons' series we publish the essential teachings of some of India's best-known spiritual teachers, along with commentaries and biographical notes. Each book will be a handy companion to help the reader along the difficult pathways of life.

Also in Aleph 'Life Lessons'

'You Are the Supreme Light': Life Lessons from Adi Shankara

'Be Present in Every Moment': Life Lessons from Moinuddin Chishti

'The Light in All is One': Life Lessons from Guru Nanak

'Live and Let Others Live': Life Lessons from Mahavira

'Looking Within': Life Lessons from Lal Ded

'Believe in Yourself': Life Lessons from Swami Vivekananda

'ONE WHO SERVES BECOMES THE MASTER'

~

LIFE LESSONS FROM

HAZRAT NIZAMUDDIN

EDITED BY

Bela Upadhyay

ALEPH

ALEPH BOOK COMPANY
An independent publishing firm
promoted by ***Rupa Publications India***

First published in India in 2021
by Aleph Book Company
7/16 Ansari Road, Daryaganj
New Delhi 110 002

ISBN: 978-81-949372-9-6

1 3 5 7 9 10 8 6 4 2

Printed at Parksons Graphics Pvt. Ltd, Mumbai

SERIES INTRODUCTION

India has produced some of the world's greatest religious leaders, sages, saints, philosophers, and spiritual thinkers. They were monks, nuns and renunciates, nationalists and reformers. No one religion had a monopoly on them. They range from Mahavira and Buddha, who lived over 2,500 years ago, to medieval saints like Chishti, Avvaiyar, and Guru Nanak, to more recent philosophers and religious icons such as Vivekananda, Ramakrishna, Saint Teresa, and many others. Each of them touched the lives of the people they lived among and the generations that followed. They inspired devotees and followers with their erudition and wisdom. The spiritual and philosophical heritage they left behind is India's gift to all Indians and the world.

Through the 'Life Lessons' series we will examine the teachings of some of India's best-known spiritual teachers. Each book will be a handy companion to help the reader along the difficult pathways of life.

Happiness and sorrow are unavoidable. The world is a place of trials and problems recur in every generation. Is suffering a necessary part of human life? How can one overcome suffering? Can hardship make a person stronger? What is happiness? Everybody wants to be happy, but how does one achieve this state? Does happiness come from vast riches and great achievements or does it come from the satisfaction of the soul? Is worldly success more important or is it fulfilment that one should seek?

These and similar questions vex every individual and have preoccupied the minds of philosophers and religious savants down the ages. The answers that these great souls found to life's conundrums occupy entire libraries worth of books and texts. This series is culled from their essential teachings and will present to readers some of the greatest truths to be found in India's spiritual heritage in a simple and accessible way. It is to be hoped that what you find here will prompt you to go deeper into the life and work of those who plumbed life's greatest mysteries.

Walking in the footsteps of these great men and women can take each of us to greater heights of knowledge, wisdom and understanding. They can teach us how to find happiness and peace and the true meaning of well-being and success. Most of all, they can teach us how to value one another and cherish the holy gift of life.

INTRODUCTION

One of the most revered Sufi saints of all time, Hazrat* Nizamuddin Auliya, of the Chishti Sufi order, spread the messages of peace and spiritual enlightenment in the late thirteenth century. Following the tradition of the Chishti order established by Moinuddin Hasan Chishti in the subcontinent in the early thirteenth

*An honorific title.

century, Sufism reached its pinnacle during Nizamuddin's time.

By the end of the twelfth century, Central Asia was in a state of ferment. This brought into the subcontinent a steady influx of travellers, poets, craftsmen and traders, as well as thoughts and ideas. Sufism was at the core of this spiritual renaissance, assimilating these ideas to evolve a unique way of life based on rejection of material possessions and the pursuit of a simple life.

Moinuddin had established his spiritual empire in the city of Ajmer. He instructed and entrusted his disciple and successor—Qutubuddin Bakhtiyar Kaki—to carry forward his teachings and philosophy. Bakhtiyar Kaki established the order in Delhi and Sufism fostered and flourished in Hazrat-e-Dilli, turning it into the epicentre of the spiritual landscape, earning it the title of 'Baees Khwajaon ki Chaukhat' (threshold of twenty-two Sufi masters).

Hazrat Nizamuddin belongs to this storied line of Chishti Sufis. Decades before his birth, his parents' families had fled the marauding Mongols from Bukhara to settle in Badaun. Nizamuddin is believed to have been born around 1238 CE to Khwaja Ahmed and Bibi Zuleikha. After losing his father at the age of five, Nizamuddin's early life was filled with hardships. But these struggles burnished his character with a stoicism and forbearance beyond his age, leading him to the quest for the real meaning and purpose of one's existence very early in life.

He completed his formal education under the

tutelage of Maulana Alauddin Usuli in Badaun. It is said that during the dastarbandi (turban-tying) ceremony, Nizamuddin placed his head with reverence at his teacher's feet after each round. Overwhelmed with this act of humility, Shaikh Ali Mawla (a well-known pious man in Badaun), who was present there, prophesied that Nizamuddin was destined for greatness.

While studying lexicography, Nizamuddin heard stories of Baba Fariduddin Ganjshakar (Bakhtiyar Kaki's disciple) that filled him with an inexplicable longing to meet the dervish. This longing grew so potent that it changed the course of his life.

According to some sources, when he was sixteen, Nizamuddin moved to Delhi with his mother and sister to pursue higher education and perhaps improve his impoverished circumstances. He approached Shaikh Najibuddin Mutawakkil, a Chishti Sufi, for assistance in gaining a vacant post of the qazi (judge of the Sharia court) of the city, but was advised by the Shaikh to become 'something else'. Incidentally, Shaikh Najibuddin Mutawakkil was Baba Farid's younger brother. But it was only after listening to a muezzin recite this verse from the Quran that Nizamuddin finally resolved to meet Baba Farid:

> Has not the time arrived
> for the Believers that
> their hearts in all humility
> should engage in the remembrance of God?*

---

*Quran, verse 57:16.

Nizamuddin took this as a sign and decided to make the journey to Ajodhan (today's Pakpattan in Pakistan). His first visit to Ajodhan to meet his spiritual master was presumably in 1265 CE. It was during his second visit, however, that Baba Farid taught him an important lesson. Nizamuddin met one of his classmates from Delhi at the inn he was staying at in Ajodhan. Seeing his impoverished state, Nizamuddin's friend remarked that such misfortune would not have befallen him had he accepted the scholarly position he had been offered. Nizamuddin remained silent but related the incident to Baba Farid the next day, asking how he should answer those who questioned his journey. Baba Farid told him to respond with this statement: 'You are not my travelling companion. Seek your own path. Get along. May prosperity be your portion in life and misfortune mine.'*

Nizamuddin imbued two other important lessons from his teacher: 'If you must incur debt, try to repay it fast,' and 'always try to please your enemies.'

Nizamuddin visited Baba Farid thrice during his lifetime (between the years of 1269 and 1271) and stayed with him for varying intervals. It was during his third visit that Nizamuddin reluctantly accepted the khilafat nama that would make him Baba Farid's spiritual successor. Nizamuddin's sole aim was to be in absolute devotion in the service of God. He felt

---

*Ziya-ul-Hasan Faruqi, *Fawa'id al-Fu'ad: Spiritual and Literary Discourses of Shaikh Nizamuddin Awliya*, New Delhi: D. K. Printworld, 1996, p. 33.

that taking on the responsibility of a master or guide would take him away from the spiritual path. To dispel his hesitation, Baba Farid said lovingly, 'Nizam, take it from me, though I do not know if I will be honoured before the Almighty, I promise not to enter heaven without your disciples.'

Nizamuddin returned to Delhi, but felt that the city did not have an accommodating environment for one seeking God. After much deliberation, he established his khanqah (hospice) at Ghiyaspur. Seven centuries ago, during the reign of Sultan Iltutmish, Ghiyaspur was a small settlement on the outskirts of the city. Located on the banks of the Yamuna, the place got its name from Sultan Ghiyasuddin Balban. Today, the area is known as Hazrat

Nizamuddin after the Sufi saint and is at the centre of bustling Delhi.

To Nizamuddin, solitude was paramount to live a life of spiritual contemplation. It was at this juncture that he received another significant life lesson from a khizr (a mystic) who joined him during an afternoon prayer. The khizr told him, 'In the first instance, one should see that one was not known to the world; but once a person had become known, he should live such a life as would protect him from feeling ashamed before the Maker on the Day of Judgement. There is no virtue and courage in keeping oneself away from people, retiring to an isolated place and contemplating God; virtue, excellence and courage lies in remaining absorbed in contemplation of God even in the midst of people.'*

Delhi, in the medieval period, was a cauldron of social, political, and cultural transformation which inherently marked Nizamuddin Auliya's religious vision with a strong sense of plurality. This helped him evolve an indigenized spirituality that transcended social and cultural differences. He strongly rejected the notion of 'zimmi'—a non-Muslim under the protection and control of a Muslim ruler. He argued: 'We are all God's zimmis under his protection only. No other human can be another's protector.'**

He was progressive in his outlook on women, who were at that time considered incapable of

*Ibid., p. 37.

**H. Sajun, *A Diary of a Disciple of Nizamuddin Auliya*, Lahore: Talifat-e-Shahidi, 2001, p. 21.

undertaking a spiritual journey. After all, it was his mother's unshakeable faith in God through extremely challenging circumstances that shaped his life. To his detractors, he would say:

Do you ask a lion
who comes out of the jungle
if it's male or female?

He would often reminisce fondly about how when they had no food to eat, his mother would lovingly tell her children, 'Today we are the guests of God'—thus reposing faith in the Maker's compassion. Her dying words had also been a reflection of her belief, 'I entrust you to the care of God.' Nizamuddin taught that it is imperative to hold no grievance in any adversity and have faith in the generosity of

God and accept whatever has been ordained by Him. Under all circumstances he held on to this sureness that he was under God's protection.

Another story shows his outlook towards women. Once, the slave of one of his disciples came to visit him along with his daughters. Delighted to meet them he said to the man, 'One who has one daughter is blessed with a barrier against Hell, and you have four. The father of four daughters is very blessed.' He believed that God increased the quantum of the livelihood of a man who had daughters and eased their circumstances.*

Nizamuddin preached that while people observed actions, God only took note of one's

---

*Faruqi, *Fawa'id al-Fu'ad*, p. 340.

intentions. He urged everyone to become like the trader who fasted for twenty-five years without either his family or his colleagues knowing about it. 'Be sincere in your khatrah (idea), azimat (resolve) and fi'l (action). When you are a beginner, it is your actions that are taken into account, but as you progress towards a higher realm of truth, you are answerable even for your thoughts.'* Only when both actions and intentions are in tandem can one thrive on this path. He gave examples of four types of believers: one, whose outwardly affairs are bright in appearance but desolate inwardly; two, whose inwardly affairs are bright but is poor and afflicted in their outward affairs;

---

*Ibid., pp. 94 and 95.

three, whose outward and inward affairs were of an evil disposition, and last, those who were blessed with spiritual purity both inwardly and outwardly. It was only this last type of believer whose inner self reflected itself through the outer self who could realize the truth. One must become like those who possess nothing and who are possessed by nothing.

The foremost decree of Nizamuddin Auliya was to embrace such acts of devotion whose rewards would benefit humankind rather than the individual. Offering prayers, going on a Haj or fasting are individualistic rituals (intransitive devotion) whose rewards are reaped only by one person. On the other hand, spreading love and compassion and praying for the peace of mankind are acts whose benefits would be enjoyed by everyone (transitive devotion). He denounced ritualistic iconoclasm and said that the highest purpose of life should be to have the generosity of a river, benevolence of the sun, and hospitality of the earth. He did not advocate a passive life of seclusion and self-mortification. Nizamuddin explained that in reality praying, fasting, singing hymns, and telling the rosary were all mere spices in a pot of water without any meat. He forbade lamentations—crying loudly, beating the chest, etc.—that were overly expressive.

He narrated a story to explain the genesis of the Sufi path (suluk). Once, a man approached a khwaja to gain knowledge about the true manner of reciting litanies and offering prayers. The khwaja sent him away, saying only, 'Do not wish for others what you would not like for yourself and wish for yourself only what you would want for others.' After a while the man came to the khwaja again and reminded him of his earlier desire. The khwaja asked the man what he had taught him on his last visit. The man could not remember. The khwaja responded, 'If you haven't followed the previous lesson how can I give you a new one?'*

Nizamuddin's life was marked by a disregard for religious orthodoxy and political hegemony. He believed he was answerable to God alone. He lived through three dynasties and a dozen rulers never succumbing to any allurement, persecution, or challenge. He turned down all

*Adapted from Faruqi, *Fawa'id al-Fu'ad,* p. 79.

attempts by Jalauddin Khalji (r. 1290–1296 CE), the founder of the Khalji dynasty to meet him. To Jalauddin's successor, Alauddin Khalji (r. 1296–1316 CE), who sought a meeting with him, Nizamuddin said, 'My khanqah has two doors. If the king enters through one, I will leave through the other door.' Despite early distrust from Alauddin, Nizamuddin eventually won him over. Two of his sons—Khidr Khan and Shadi Khan—were even initiated into his discipleship. But another son, Qutubuddin Mubarak (r. 1316–1320 CE) ascended the throne, and it was during his reign that Nizamuddin faced the most malicious display of political power. The king placed a bounty on Nizamuddin's life, ordered him to offer his Friday prayers at the Masjid-i-Mirri, banned his nobles and state officials from visiting Nizamuddin's hospice in the hope that it would stop the flow of charity and, in one of his most obnoxious moves to force the Shaikh to toe the line, introduced a practice whereby all distinguished citizens of the city had to place their greetings at the king's palace after the sighting of the moon of the new month. The Chishtis believed that God was the only one to whom obeisance must be paid. Nizamuddin dealt with all these incidents with stoic indifference. He was also at loggerheads with the founder of the Tughluq dynasty—Ghiyasuddin Tughluq (r. 1320–1325 CE). They disagreed on two main issues—on Sama—the Sufi practice of gathering to listen to religious poetry that is often accompanied by ecstatic dancing and musical instruments. Nizamuddin was a believer in the power of music to achieve oneness with God whereas music was prohibited in Islam. The sultan was also unhappy that Nizamuddin had given away in charity the money he had received as a gift from the sultan's predecessor.

Towards the end of his life, when Nizamuddin knew the time of his departure from this world was near he stopped eating. If he were offered food, he would say, 'How can one relish any food when one is looking forward to meeting the Maker?' When he became weaker and was requested to take medicine, he quoted his disciple, Amir Khusro: 'To the victim of divine love there is no other remedy except meeting his Beloved.' A day before his death, he ordered his attendants to distribute everything in the kitchen so that he would not have to give an account of the same before God. Just before his death he handed over the traditional sacred relics which he had received from his master, Baba Fariduddin, to Nasiruddin Chiragh Dehlavi, his successor, with the words, 'You must stay in Delhi and suffer the persecution of the people.' He departed from this mortal world in 1325 CE on 3 April.

Throughout his life Nizamuddin dedicated himself to the service of the Maker and his creations and left an indelible mark that has served as the spiritual axis of the city through the centuries. The legacy of Mehboob-e-Elahi (Beloved of God), Sultan-al-Mashaikh (king amongst Sufis), Jag Ujjare (Light of the World) and Dastageer-e-do-Jahan (Holder of two worlds) is embedded in our living memory as a beacon of beneficence. He is also called Qutb-e-Dehli by his devotees who consider him an intercessor between them and the Maker. Once a disgruntled royal official, weary of the crowds that thronged his khanqah asked him, 'What is it that you try to achieve? Do you want to make them like you?' He had replied in his incomparable style: 'I do not want to make them like me. I want to make them better than I am!'

THE PRINCIPLES OF SUFISM

Love for the Creator is the overarching essence of Sufism. Nizamuddin stressed that the path to mystical love has to be tread with certitude. To keep the soul free from the evils of the physical world and attachment to material possessions one should not be occupied by any profession. Instead one should place implicit trust in God to provide for your subsistence. He opposed serving any master other than God.

He laid down strict injunctions regarding charity. Only wealth earned through righteous means could be given in charity. The intention should be sincere, it given with humility without any expectation of recognition. No matter how pitiful the circumstances were, the laws of Sufism dictated never to ask for charity. He strictly forbade his followers from putting aside for the next day what was received in charity and urged his followers to distribute everything among the poor and needy.

Tariqah (the Sufi path) to realizing the truth contained many stations—zikr (remembrance of God), tawba (penitence), nafs (conquering the carnal self), tasadduq (charity), rizq (sustenance), sabr (patience), wazu (purity of body), qinaat (contentment) and fakr (a life of wilful poverty lived with contentment). After achieving several dimensions of devotion, the worldly and spiritual realms of one's being would be illuminated leading to spiritual sublimation. This last stage haqiqah (Reality) contained fanaa (annihilation of ego), sahur (wakefulness), sidq (absolute truth), tawakkul (absolute trust), tasawwuf (Sufi mysticism), tark-i-duniya (renunciation), zakat (purification of thoughts), and zuhd (an act of doing without).

The pursuit of knowledge should encompass the senses, reason, and divine intelligence. To reach this realm was a persistent search and one should not stop at the realm of reason by marvelling at the mysticism of the acquired knowledge. Knowledge belongs to the one whose actions correspond with what he knows. Nizamuddin reiterated that appearance and reality are reflections of each other. He strongly opposed the display of one's spiritual accomplishments.

He taught that penitence is intrinsic to this path of Sufism. Nizamuddin asked his followers to be steadfast in their repentance of sins. Nizamuddin believed that the doors of spirituality were always open to those who atoned sincerely. However, repentance is only the beginning and the process would be incomplete if the seeker did not learn to forgive. It is equally important to free our heart of bitterness and negative feelings and not answer evil with evil—this will only lead to unending conflict and disorder in society. To forgive, one needs to deal with anger in the right way. Teach yourself not to be affected by the actions of others.

A spiritual traveller aims at perfection and purification. While external purification suffices for ritualistic devotion, internal purification means a purging of all the senses, the heart, reason, and soul. Once, a woman asked Nizamuddin if it was possible to continue with the devotional rituals during the time of menstruation. Touched by her resolute love for God he told her not to worry if the prayer mat gets stained. What was important was her purity in remembering and invoking the name of the

Maker. Ablutions only clean the body. It is the purity of thoughts that cleanses the soul.

He understood that there would be times when one might dither from his trust in the Maker but he asked seekers to be hopeful of a return to the path as long as one does not become hostile.

Explaining the virtues of contentment and sacrifice, Nizamuddin explains the beauty of detachment from worldly possessions using a pearl as a metaphor:

> Everyday God displays a new grandeur. When one grandeur is being manifested he bestows something from one person to another and when the second facet of his grandeur is being displayed he returns the

thing from the second person to the first one. These are like pearls which are born in seashells. The rain bearing clouds send a shower. The drops of rain falling into a seashell become a pearl and drops falling into a snake's mouth become venom. Today the pearls that were made by rain bearing clouds were taken out of the sea by divers, sold by traders, bought by rich people and taken away by kings. From the kings these pearls would reach a dervish. The dervish has no room in his heart for them since it is already filled with God's lustrous pearls. So remember that these pearls may be yours but you should never belong to them because every man is born for God and the world is created for him.

> We should give away the pearls and they will reach where they started from as we have been given a heart so that we may light the love of God in them and dispel all darkness.*

He taught that when friends arrive, food should be offered without any discrimination. When God has not discriminated amongst his creations who are we to do so? Nizamuddin observed very strict etiquettes of eating. Nobody should be asked whether they are fasting or not. He reasoned that if one is fasting and reveals it, his spirituality which was abstruse becomes known and is taken as an exhibition of devotion; if one conceals it, he lies; if one lies that he is fasting

---

*Sajun, *A Diary of a Disciple of Nizamuddin Auliya*, pp. 58–59.

he is hypocritical and if one keeps his silence the act is considered a humiliation of the host. He was a frugal eater and fasted very often. He would often pretend to eat so that those with whom he shared his meals would not go hungry on his behalf. Sometimes half-chewed morsels were found in his bowl. He would ask how he could enjoy his food when so many people had gone to bed hungry.

One of the greatest gifts that Nizamuddin gave society was encouraging his disciple Amir Khusro to experiment with language and music. He was a believer in the use of music in spiritual experiences. He believed that music could liberate a listener and place him in intimacy with God. Khusro is considered the father of Qawwali. Even today, Qawwali performances are held at the Nizamuddin Dargah, attracting large crowds of people. The use of song and dance in religious practices was a contentious issue, but Nizamuddin argued that its purpose defined its morality—real Sama was related to compassion.

The reason behind his universal popularity was his tolerance of all irrespective of their religion, caste, and socio-economic background. He learned from his Hindu disciples and yogis about Hindu ideals of spirituality. His hospice drew large numbers of followers because he never turned away anyone seeking salvation, thus truly becoming the tree that Baba Fariduddin had blessed him to be, under whose soothing shadow people would find comfort. During a spiritual gathering he once said, 'Where do we have enough time to ponder over what is a Hindu belief and what is a Muslim belief? We are immersed in this wonder of how the ocean is held within the bubble and that the heart has no room for anything besides love.... We are absorbed in external awareness and forget our internal awareness. We are independent and we are restricted too. We exist and are non-existent. We are of use and yet useless. All these are manifestations of one single zaat (soul).*

He had strong views on the impropriety of displaying one's miraculous powers or karamah. The spiritual journey was made up of a hundred stages and karamah was the seventeenth stage, so how could one cover the rest of the path if one

---

*H. Sajun, *A Diary of a Disciple of Nizamuddin Auliya*, pp. 46–47.

stopped and revelled in one's own achievement? He felt that understanding the power that came with miracles needed a deeper knowledge of its purpose.

Replacing religious parochialism with practical aspects and an ideology of service to humanity has led to Nizamuddin's everlasting legacy. He survived through a turbulent fourteenth century that saw political upheavals, social churning and multiple invasions. His presence was like an oasis of hope, love and comfort in those times and even today his dargah offers solace to anyone who comes in search of acceptance and guidance. His believers feel he makes them acceptable in God's eyes despite their unworthiness. They believe in his protection. His expansive kindness during his lifetime is a legacy carried on by his descendants—the Nizami Chishti order—making him an institution where generosity still flows freely.

I

THE ILLUSION

CONQUER YOUR LOWER SELF

Without humility,
the soil of hope is unwatered.

Wish for others only what you wish for yourself.
Do not approve of those deeds in yourself
when you disapprove of them in others.

Separate yourself from desires.
Awake to the magnificence before you.

A heart which is consumed with love of the Beloved
can never hold any malice.

Walk with fortitude on this path
denounce lust and desire.
That is the way to God.

If one betrays the trust of someone by revealing their secret,
he will never be given any secrets to keep again.

You consider yourself
to be good and pious?
You cannot be
in a worse state

on the path to the absolute truth.

Words and wisdom are both worthless
if they are nothing but a means to manipulate
and flatter others.

Revealing the ill deeds of someone:
does it make you more virtuous?

Follow my actions.
Merely imitating my countenance is useless.

Honesty alone will
lead to lasting fame.
Glorious cities have
perished to dishonesty.

Conquer your ego.
Pray to become selfless and
see the path illuminate before you.

There is no glory in
displaying your spiritual achievements.

The flame of love
will only kindle a heart
that is pure and purged of any evil.

A mortal life is worthless.
It should not be trusted
to bequeath us any benefit.
You are foolish
if you spend this state of transience
in negligence of your duties towards God.

You are nothing but an impostor
who pretends to be a friend of God.
You can continue on the path of devotion
only if you rid yourself
of every attachment.
Look at you, you still engage
in the pleasures of the world.

In arguments and conversations
there should be no place for
anger, pride, and arrogance
even if you are among friends.

One's faith is incomplete
until all worldly desires
and attachments mean
the same as a piece of stone.

Pray to God!
Surrender to the remembrance of His name.
He will absolve you of your vanity.
In this journey, egoistical and self-seeking people
can never attain spiritual sublimation.

All those possessions which are more than
what you need are worldly.
All the prayers offered
and devoutness observed by you
with an intention to serve the self
are worldly.
All actions in the fulfilment of one's
responsibilities
towards one's family
appear to be worldly—
however, they are not.

II

THE PATH

SURRENDER YOUR HEART TO GOD

It is the love of God
that is the absolute purpose
behind the creation of life.
So surrender your heart
to the Maker in complete allegiance.

God is the reliever;
God is the healer;
God is bountiful.

God will hold you to be his friend
if you have
the generosity of a river,
the benevolence of the Sun and
the hospitality of the Earth.

Be like the man
who brings out the water
from the depth of the well and
gives life to a parched piece of land.
Immerse yourself
in the remembrance of God.
Discharge and draw your breath
repeating God's name
and you will see
the land of your soul bloom.

Supplication,
observing a fast,
telling the rosary,
going on Haj
are all acts of devotion.
The rewards for this
will benefit you personally.
But when you offer your love and
keep your heart generous
towards mankind—
these acts of devotion.
benefit all.

Even a little devoutness
is worthy if
it is sincere and honest.

Give up a despicable thing
so as to be rewarded
with an honourable one.

Only true love
can arouse deep feelings.
Words spoken without any experience of love
are thus only mere words.

You may live in a city,
you may live in a desert.
God's love will not change
like the seasons
if He has truly blessed you.

If you believe you can never be impure.
Go forward on the path of God in whatever

appearance you came in.
One with a taste of unquestionable devotion can never feel attracted to the mundane in life.
Such a person will embrace death with sincerity.

ONE WHO SERVES BECOMES THE MASTER

Silence is the language that pious men
converse in.

Your first effort should be to remain hidden
to the world.
But if you become known, then courage
does not lie in seclusion from the world.
Courage is remaining in God's remembrance
even while being engaged with the world.

Do not consider that being a master
or being a servant
is an obstacle in the way of God.
In this journey
there will be many hardships.
If you withstand
the ordeals of the world of love
you will be rewarded.

For the purification of the soul,
embrace a life of
little speech,
little food,
little sleep, and
little engagement with the world.

Do not worry if you are deprived
of all your worldly possessions.
They are transient.
The only permanence
is the love of God.
Seek only that.

Saying that you don't want the world is in
reality expressing a longing for it.
If you possess the world, spend it on those
who need it.
If you do not possess it, reconcile to your
situation.
Your contentment should be in the
tranquillity
of this state of non-being.

To dedicate your entire life
in the service of God
may be difficult in the beginning.
Pursue the path with utmost sincerity
and devoutness.
Your journey will become fruitful.
This divine grace is His blessing.

Do not go from door to door
in pursuit of His love.
Be firm
and hold onto one place.
What you seek shall come to you.

We walk in different directions
trying to reach the same goal.
Some fail in this journey.

Some succeed.
If only we would unite
and walk along the same path
in one direction
will we all not reach our destination?

Do not try to occupy the place
that you wish for.
Be seated wherever you find room.
In the house of God
this is how
one should conduct oneself.

There are many keys
to unlock the door
of spiritual perfection.
Possess all of them.

If one key fails to open the door,
others will.

One who serves becomes the master.
Be the one to serve.
Only servitude will lead you
to being served in turn.

One may have differences
of opinion and
a different point of view.
Never express anger
when sitting with friends
or even with strangers.

Honour and dignity are acquired with
knowledge.

With devotion and worship we come closer
to experiencing God's generosity.
It is at this stage that we need a guide.
He will break our illusions of perfection
and teach us the impermanence of reason.
His guidance will liberate you
and reveal the truth to you.

Do not become ill disposed
towards someone
just because he speaks ill of you.

Be patient:
if the pen inscribing your accomplishments is
slow and sluggish,
it means that your work is still incomplete.
Persevere on the path.

Do not run from one door to another.
Hold on to one master.
Let him guide your path.

Only fasting can subjugate desires.
Fasting needs patience.
Patience needs belief.
Belief needs truth.

BE GENEROUS

You who make me grieve,
may your comforts grow.
You who are not my friend,
may God be your friend.

If one places thorns
in retaliation to another,
then there will be no flowers,
only thorns.

Keep doing good deeds.

Attain God's favour.
Remember that the record of your actions
will be read by Him
in the next world.

Pray for peace within yourself.
Whoever does this,
whatever their circumstances
they will find rest.

He who calls himself my enemy puts thorns
in my way.
I wish for his garden to bloom,
and let all the flowers in that garden be
without thorns.

Knowledge is a wealth and every wealth has its zakat*
Action is the tax levied on knowledge.

God created everyone equal.
How can you discriminate in your service?

If there is nothing to offer, serve a cup of water.
No visitor should leave without being offered anything.

Do not ask for anything,
take what is given to you.
Keep what you need,

---

*Tax paid on one's wealth, one of the pillars of Islam.

give the rest away to someone who needs it.

If prosperity favours you,
spend that wealth
for the benefit of others. By doing so
you ensure that it never lessens.
If ever it was to slip out of your hands
do not have your eye on it.
It has no permanence.

Drink after everyone
has quenched their thirst.
Eat not before others have.

Your wealth is as useless as a piece of stone
if it is not shared with those who are less
fortunate.

Never submit to anger
Conquer it with forgiveness.

There is no honour in revealing the faults of others.
Search within yourself first—did you find the fault in yourself?
If you are guilty of a similar weakness, feel ashamed of deprecating others.
If you are free from the fault,
be grateful that God kept you
protected from it.

Are you the one who asks the gardener to close the gates of the garden
when you and your Beloved (God) are inside?
Open the gates to all,

let everyone bask in God's benediction.

Forgive those who slander you.
Dispel the darkness of ill-will from your heart.
Belong to everyone,
abandon all the bitterness you have for anyone who speaks ill of you.

Kindness and forgiveness are the virtues to be practised to perfection.
When one prays it should be
for the salvation of all.
Raise your spirit to a higher level of consciousness.

No man is a slave of another.
Free them to free yourself.

If you have given away something in charity,
do not wish for it to be returned.

Learn to serve
rather than be a master.
Do not subject others to your will
and choice, rather submit
to the will and choice of others.

With time knowledge and faith will perish.
It is only the domain of compassion that is
timeless.

God displays his munificence
in a heart that embodies goodness.

III

THE TRUTH

BE ABSOLUTE IN YOUR TRUST

Stay not with those who have never known
the ordeals of love.
Live with those who have surrendered to it
and chosen to experience
the pangs of suffering with humility.

Have faith in God's will.
A dua (prayer) is only
to comfort the heart.
He gives us what is in our interest.

Always seek strength from your heart.
Your words will become stronger as the heart
is guided by God.

Are you a mountain?
If every wind makes you quiver
like a straw, you are not worthy
of being even a straw.

God is generous.
But you should remember that these struggles
in your endeavour
will be your achievement.

If you seek the key to peace and happiness,
accept God's will.

God sustains you,
nourishes you
and nurtures you
from above.
Then why build a house
on this earth?
Are you an ant, a spider, or a bee?

CHALLENGE YOURSELF

Be honest in your repentance.
Take a solemn promise
to abstain
from the corruptions of the world.
Your path of return to God
will open again.

In the name of the piety of righteous men,
may I be forgiven my sins.
If I am not a sinner
then may I be counted as one of them.

Criticize yourself.
Challenge yourself.
It will give you rewards
worth many years of devotion.

If you meet a sinner today
do not take pride in yourself.
Tomorrow, he might be on God's path
while you might have been distracted
from it.
So never consider yourself
better than anyone
you meet on this path.

A yarn which repeatedly breaks
while weaving
becomes stronger

every time it is joined
than one which remains unbroken.
Likewise, one who has committed a sin
and is repentant
is superior to the one
who has committed none.

If you feed your desires, they grow.
Starve them and they diminish.
Eliminate them and you receive everything.

A sincere atonement of a sin
and having committed none at all
are equal in the eyes of God.

REALIZE THE TRUTH

You keep searching for the fragrance
that is already under your gilm.*
It is your miserable circumstances
that keep the musk hidden from you.

Have good faith
and do not chase
after knowing everything.

Love needs no consultation.

---

*A garment made from goat's wool, worn by mendicants.

Love needs no permission.
Love needs only sincerity.

Whatever good or evil
has been committed by you
is the fulfilment of the will of God.
He is the creator of all things.
Thus, what one is afflicted with
comes from Him,
then why this sadness and distress?

It is God who helps me through knowledge
It is he who adorns me with fortitude.

Consciousness of the non-being will make
you a lion.
Without that you are a mere speck of dust.

It is wise to be forewarned
of the outcome of deeds
in opposition to piety,
righteousness, and generosity.
Learn from the abjection of those
who have indulged in ill deeds.

Do nothing for the sake of any desire.
Seek no pleasure or satisfaction
from your actions.
Be a man of God—
every intention of yours
should be for the sake of God.

It is God's blessing,
an intercession of the Prophet,
a favour from your teacher—

if any good deed that comes from you
serves someone.
In the same way—any evil
that comes forth from you
is to be considered your misfortune.

Logic cannot hold love.
It can only weave a web of trickery.
Reject it, quickly.

To live as a recluse
and strip oneself to the skin
is not true renunciation.
If one lives in this world,
takes food as usual
and wears proper clothes
but is content with whatever he has,

has no greed to accumulate
and is not attached
to the things of the world
is a true renunciate.

The fox went forward to claw the lion
and faced his own punishment.
Why did it not stay in its place?

If you claim
that anything said or done by you
was just because of a revelation
and miracle,
you would render yourself
to be a juggler's donkey.
Do not let your carnal self
feel inflated and be deluded

to think that you have become
something great.

Seek the world in a limited way
if you have a desire for it at all.
Do not exert yourself
in its pursuit.
Learn from the plight of others
and be forewarned
of the consequences
of improper deeds.

To be a good student
take food that you like
at most once a day,
so that there is place
left for knowledge.

Do not be irregular
on the path of learning.

When you present yourself before God,
place your head on the ground.
No one is more enlightened
than the one whose ego is subdued.

If you do not have
the heart of a lion,
do not walk
on the path of love.

The dust of his doorstep
is the right thing to apply
if the surmah does not show beauty
of the eye.

Walking on the path of knowledge,
sit with a learned man and listen to him.
Heaven will be your abode.

Spiritual intoxication is inferior to spiritual continence.

In the way of God, men and women are equally endowed in discipline and power.

Corrupt means of earning a livelihood
can never earn you any spiritual wealth.

Remember when the Day of Judgement comes,
your accounts will be settled in accordance to how you have earned.
Dubious earnings will only invite punishment.

While praying
think only of God's mercy.
Think neither of your remorse nor of sins committed.

How can the love for carnal desires and the love for God dwell in one heart?

Do not forsake the world.
Face their admonishment and their judgement.

God bestows man
with justice and generosity.
Man's kinship is based on justice,
favour, and oppression.

Love of God should be the only inspiration
when we call out his name.
Pray not because of the fear of hell and
temptation for heaven.

To treat grown-ups with love,
learn to love children.

Burn a heap of vices with
a single particle of honesty.

Whatever is recited
during a prayer
should guide the heart on the path of
attainment of higher wisdom.

Denounce the desires
that cage you and free yourself,
see how a thousand favourites
sit before you.

Who is there
who has not saved his skin
from evil.
Who is there
whom the beast
has not attempted to devour?

Unveiling and mysteries of the Divine
are the curtains of the way.
In steadfastness
there is love
and it is love

that has a right to intervene.

One who is restless to be known to the world
will fall into oblivion soon.
While the one who kept his name and achievements hidden
will be known throughout.

Men of God drink from infinite streams of knowledge.
Their thirst for the glory of wisdom is unquenchable.

A master should only guide a disciple's behaviour
through subtle hints.

Never should he be open in his
admonishment.

Miracles obfuscate the view.
They cloud our reality.

In a spiritual journey
there is no difference
between a man and a woman.
Do you ask a lion
who comes out of the jungle
if it's male or female?
They are equally accomplished
and capable of discipline,
power and talent.

Come and meet me in the tavern,
delight in the intoxication of the love of the Beloved.
There are no barriers.
You can settle here permanently.

Though you may be profane—
if you do not indulge
in finding fault with others,
you are a person of virtue.
Though you may be bad—
if you avoid speaking ill of others,
you are a person with goodness.

I am loved by people
only because they know
I am Your servant and Your slave.

This is a favour
that has been bestowed upon me
like a blessing.
If not for this,
I'm nothing.

A verse written and sung
with the intention of self-gain
is nothing but farcical
and will only cause ridicule.
Only a verse
that is a true reflection of the purity
of the mystical experience
will give joy to the listener.

Friends who enjoy drinks with you

in the garden of beauty
and pleasure
are indeed your enemies.

You are appointed
to look after the garden,
you cannot taste the fruits
to know which one is sweet
and which one sour.

Abstinence from food for a long time
is in fact like having never kept a fast
and never having broken it.

Is it not vicious that as you near your end
you fall in love with God?
Know that on the Day of Judgement

deeds committed by you in your youth
will be under question.

To accomplish—
you need to begin!

IV

THE LIBERATION

THE PATH TO RENUNCIATION

The path to achieving absolute renunciation
requires—not indulging in a profession
for sustenance;
not asking for a loan;
concealing difficulties
and not seeking any help
even if you have been starving for a week;
not saving for tomorrow;
not praying to God
to wish harm on someone else.

Keep your wealth hidden under the cloth of
renunciation.
Veil your spiritual journey and its rewards
from the eyes of those whose intentions are
impure.

Even if the world assures you that you would
not be condemned,
do not accept it.
This world with all its limitations and
attachments
is unacceptable even to God.

After one's consciousness is awakened
one becomes like a bare tree,
prepared to welcome new leaves.

ONE WHO KNOWS HIMSELF KNOWS GOD

The abundance of ambitions
and the ability to control
one's spiritual secrets
make one worthy
of the state of consciousness.

It is the soul
that first attains perfection
through realization
and liberation

from all attachments.
It then attracts the heart
to this state of perfection
and in turn the heart
then guides the body
to a state of perfection.

In misery I seek the way to your abode.
Tears decorate my face
I die with your name on my lips.

In the pain of separation
I will destroy myself.
I keep my eyes fixed on my Beloved
in the hope of meeting him.
I will not waver in my quest of a union with
him.

The soul is neither internal
nor external
of our material form.
It is neither a constant
nor a motion.
Knowledge of the soul
is knowledge of God.
One who knows himself
knows God.

One man said:
'I'll perform my prayers at Mecca.'
The second man said:
'I'll pray at Medina.'
Third man said:

'I'll pray at Bait-al-Muqqadas*.'
The fourth said:
'I'll offer my prayers at the feet of my teacher.'
So, tell me now:
who is my true lover?

I do not want anything from you,
nor have I ever entertained
any expectation from you.
I'm determined
not to extend my palms
before anyone.
Now, permit me
not to draw my leg back.

---

*Jerusalem.

Do not fear the men of the Invisible realm
when they call out your name.
Leave with them.
The place they take you is one of bliss.

One who is immersed in the sight of the Beloved
can never experience any grief.

God has shown me everything.
His light touches me, illuminating me from within
and appearing on the outside like a bed of roses.

Enduring the condemnable
without any complaint is patience.

Not feeling the condemnable
as if it had never existed is quietism.

To men of consciousness God shows the
invisible.
These men never reveal what they hear,
what they see and what they know.
Their lips are sealed about the faults of
others.

To see what lies beyond and beneath the
realm of the hidden
cleanse your body,
purify your thoughts,
love your master, and
always remain in the contemplation of the
Maker.